Peace and contentment evermore abide
In your quaint hamlet by the Brandywine!

"Our Old Village" by John Russell Hayes

Chadds Ford

History, Heroes and Landmarks

Written and Photographed by
Carla Westerman

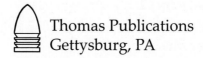
Thomas Publications
Gettysburg, PA

Maps by Chris Jones

Cover design by Laura Westerman Koster

Cover illustration: John Chads springhouse

Illustration on page 4: Miss Gratz by Clayton Bright,
Brandywine River Museum.

Contents

Introduction 7

Chapter 1: Colonial Chadds Ford 9

Chapter 2: Chadds Ford Painters and Poets 32

Chapter 3: Chadds Ford Village 44

Chapter 4: Chadds Ford Today 62

Chadds Ford Information 76

Sources and Further Reading 77

Maps

Chadds Ford Village 6

Battle of Brandywine Overview 20

Top Five Battle Sites 21

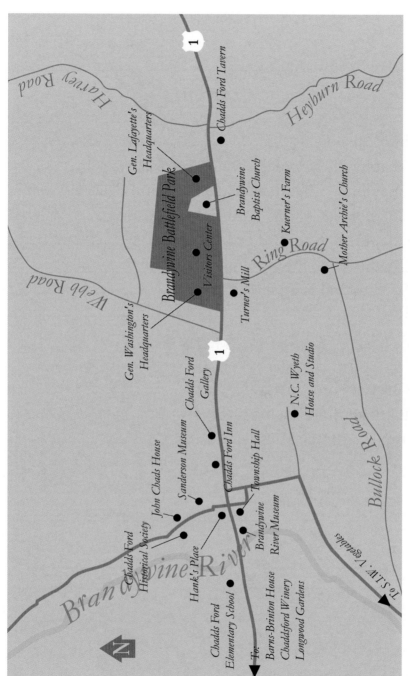

1

Chadds Ford Tavern

Harvey Road

Heyburn Road

Gen. Lafayette's Headquarters

Brandywine Battlefield Park

Brandywine Baptist Church

Kuerner's Farm

Mother Archie's Church

Visitors Center

Webb Road

Ring Road

Turner's Mill

Gen. Washington's Headquarters

1

Chadds Ford Gallery

N.C. Wyeth House and Studio

Bullock Road

Sanderson Museum

Chadds Ford Inn

Township Hall

John Chads House

Brandywine River Museum

To S.W. Vegetables

Chadds Ford Historical Society

Hank's Place

Brandywine River

Chadds Ford Elementary School

To:
Barns-Brinton House
Chaddsford Winery
Longwood Gardens

N

Chadds Ford

6

Introduction

*C*hadds Ford — a name that conjures up images of Wyeth art, the Brandywine River, Revolutionary soldiers on the march and pastoral landscapes dotted with old stone houses and inns. Nestled in the heart of the historic Brandywine Valley, tiny Chadds Ford is just a dot on the map of southeastern Pennsylvania about 30 miles from Philadelphia. Yet every year thousands of visitors find their way to this bucolic area that has become a magnet for art and history enthusiasts.

Chadds Ford's identity has been forged over the course of more than 300 years with each century leaving an imprint and legacy. In the late 1600s English colonists began settling on the fertile land by the Brandywine that was part of William Penn's land grant. In the 1700s the rural Quaker hamlet found itself in the path of the largest land battle of the American Revolution. During the 1800s Chadds Ford served as a village hub for surrounding farms as well as a fashionable summer destination for city dwellers.

Native Americans fished and canoed in its waters, George Washington stood on its banks and an artistic tradition derives its name from the Brandywine.

7

Traveling south on Creek Road.

In the twentieth century its picturesque riverside setting nurtured the development of the distinctive Brandywine School of painting. Today Chadds Ford has become a sought-after residential address as well as a tourist destination known for its cultural attractions.

Despite the inevitable march of progress, Chadds Ford's narrow back roads still wind through unspoiled landscapes and past river bends immortalized in Andrew Wyeth's paintings. With stellar attractions such as the Brandywine River Museum and Brandywine Battlefield Park plus the presence of the Wyeth family of artists, this quiet enclave seems to attract visitors without even trying. No large billboards announce Chadds Ford — just a discreet sign or two alerts the driver that he has arrived.

The story of Chadds Ford is told in these pages through its historical and cultural landmarks, its community events and the words of its people. Chadds Ford is small — the township is a little more than eight square miles — so all places described are within a few miles of each other.

Colonial Chadds Ford

A drive along the back roads of Chadds Ford reveals why history and tradition play an important role here. The historic landscape — houses and barns in unspoiled settings — hints at what life was like for previous generations and provides a sense of continuity with the past. The story of Chadds Ford, like many colonial Pennsylvania communities, began with a few intrepid settlers, the lure of economic opportunity and religious freedom, and close ties to England. After America severed those ties in 1776, Chadds Ford found itself engulfed in George Washington's defense at Brandywine — a battle that left devastation and a rich historical legacy in its wake.

The Brandywine River

The Brandywine is Chadds Ford's lifeblood, its most important natural resource, its reason for existing. Some say the origin of its poetic name comes from the Dutch word for brandy, "brandewijn." A Dutch ship laden with barrels of brandy reportedly wrecked at the mouth of the river in 1655 spilling its precious cargo and christening the stream.

The name more likely came from an early Dutch settler named Andrew Braindwinde. The Lenni-Lenape Indians who were living along its riverbanks when the first Europeans arrived called it "Wawaset."

As in colonial times, the center of Chadds Ford today is where the Brandywine meets U.S. Route 1, once known as "Ye Great Road to Nottingham." Laid out in 1707, the highway became a major route connecting Philadelphia to Baltimore along America's eastern coast.

Travelers arriving at the riverbank on horseback or hauling a wagon often needed help to negotiate the crossing. Flooding or icy conditions made the fording especially treacherous. An enterprising local farmer named John Chads started a ferry service and the crossing became known as "Chad's Ford."

Chads used a cable system to pull a large flat-bottomed boat across the stream and landing docks were built on either side.

John Chads ferried people, animals and wagons across the stream.

The crossing is believed to have been located north of the present Route 1 bridge, not far from Chads' house. Chads asked the county to fix a fee schedule so that he would not have to negotiate a price with each customer.

Every horse and Rider, four pence.

Every single person on foot, three pence, if more, two pence each.

Every ox, cow or heifer, four pence each.

Every sheep, one penny.

Every Hog, three half pence.

Every Coach, waggon or Cart, one shilling and six pence.

Fee schedule established for Chads' Ferry by the Court of Quarter Sessions in 1737

Artist Andrew Wyeth has often depicted the Brandywine in the bleakness of winter — also the best time to appreciate the breadth of the stream.

Chads saw potential in the increasing commercial traffic along the route and opened a tavern to serve his passengers and neighbors. Ferry service across the Brandywine continued until the first bridge at Chadds Ford was built in 1828.

The Brandywine springs from the Welsh Mountains of northwestern Chester County near Honeybrook and flows for about 60 miles in a south-easterly direction through Pennsylvania and into Dela-ware. As it winds its way through meadow, marsh and woodlands, the Brandywine changes in size, character and appearance. Some maps call it a creek, others a river; local residents refer to it both ways. In Chadds Ford the river travels in a serpentine path alongside Creek Road offering unspoiled vistas with each turn in the road. Several miles north of Chadds Ford the stream splits into two: the small west branch coming from Coatesville and the east flowing through Downingtown.

The lower Brandywine in Delaware has the swiftest currents and once powered numerous mills including the du Pont family gunpowder works. Below Wilmington it joins with the Christina River and empties into the Delaware River.

As idyllic as the Brandywine looks on a sunny day, the river can become a dangerous torrent during heavy rains, often flood-ing low-lying roads and sometimes covering Route 1. During a storm in 1999, the river surged over its banks and floodwaters crept halfway up the windows of the Brandywine River Museum's lower level.

❖ *Insider's Tip:* To stand on the banks of the Brandywine, go to the Brandywine River Museum on U.S. Route 1, just west of Creek Road. Next to the parking lot the mile-long River Trail offers a pleasant walk along the riverbanks passing under the Route 1 bridge and leading to the Chadds Ford Historical Society on Creek Road. For a different vantage point, rent a canoe or an inner tube and float down the stream. Local canoe companies provide equipment and shuttle customers upstream or meet them downstream.

John Chads House

1719 Creek Road, 0.25 mile north of Route 1, opposite the Chadds Ford Historical Society.
Info: (610) 388-7376; www.chaddsfordhistory.org

Perched on a hillside above the Brandywine, the John Chads House is one of the oldest buildings in Chadds Ford. It is also the home of its namesake — ferryman John Chads. In 1725 Chads built the bluestone house on land inherited from his parents. This was a substantial house for the times but in keeping with Quaker tradition, simple and unpretentious. The home's features suggest that Chads was a person of moderate wealth and status in the community.

Born in 1697, Chads was the son of Quaker colonists who had immigrated from Wiltshire, England, to take advantage of William Penn's land grant opportunities in southeastern Pennsylvania. The industrious younger Chads farmed the 500-acre riverfront property and operated a tavern in addition to his ferry business — a telling example of how immigrant Quaker families quickly prospered in the fertile Brandywine Valley.

Confusion over the spelling of names exists because Chads shortened his family name which was Chadsey. The river crossing where he operated his ferry business eventually became known as Chadds Ford, spelled with two d's.

A wonderful example of an early Quaker country home, the solidly-built house has two bedrooms upstairs, two rooms on the main floor and a lower level kitchen with a beehive oven. Chads lived in the house with his wife Elizabeth until his death in 1760.

Home of the ferryman who is Chadds Ford's namesake.

The couple had no children and Elizabeth stayed on in the house by herself for 30 more years.

During the Battle of Brandywine, the 67-year-old widow Elizabeth not only witnessed the fighting but found herself directly in the line of fire. Washington had positioned his artillery on the steep embankment by the Chads house facing British forces across the river. Though the house was spared, it is thought that cannon fire caused damage to the spring house below.

Breadbaking in the beehive oven and tours by guides in period costume are held May to September and by appointment.

> *To protect her valued possessions during the battle, Elizabeth "buried Her Silver Spoons Daily in her Packet [pocket] until the Danger was over."*

The William Brinton 1704 House

21 Oakland Road, 0.3 mile south of Dilworthtown.
Info: (610) 399-0913; www.brintonfamily.org

A tribute to the building skills of early settlers is the number of 18th-century homesteads still standing in Chadds Ford today. One of the most distinctive is the William Brinton 1704 House which has been restored by Brinton family members whose ancestors emigrated from Birmingham, England more than 300 years ago.

With graceful leaded-glass windows and stone walls twenty-two inches thick, this was likely the finest house in colonial Chadds Ford. William Brinton built the house in 1704, incorporating elements of medieval design from his native England.

The Brinton family saga illustrates the risks and rewards experienced by early settlers coming to America. William Brinton was 14 years old when he sailed to America with his Quaker parents in 1684. Instead of settling in an established town like Philadelphia, the family traveled out to the frontier of Chester County and spent the first winter living in a cave near what is now Route 202. The first English settlers to the area, they might have starved if not for food supplied by the Lenape Indians.

William Brinton, who spent his first winter in America living in a cave with his parents, built this elegant home.

The elder Brinton and William built a wood plank cabin on a 450-acre land grant from William Penn and began farming. They called their new home Birmingham after the English town they had left in search of religious freedom.

William married in 1690 and continued to live in the family cabin until he built the larger house to accommodate his wife and six children. As the family prospered, its land holdings increased to 1000 acres.

The Brinton home was ransacked by British soldiers after the Battle of Brandywine. The family lost many of its possessions, including its only mirror.

In 1954 Brinton family descendants restored their ancestral home and opened the house to visitors. It is furnished with period pieces and family heirlooms based on room-by-room inventories taken at the death of William Brinton in 1751.

❖ *Insider's Tip:* A historical marker identifies the burial place of William Brinton Sr. and his wife Ann, both of whom died before their son built the 1704 house. It is located on the east side of Route 202 behind a motel building, a half-mile north of Oakland Road.

Barns-Brinton House

Route 1, 1.8 miles west of Creek Road, enter at traffic light at Pond's Edge Drive.
Info: (610) 388-7376; www.chaddsfordhistory.org

Taverns and inns dotted the landscape in the 1700s providing shelter for travelers and a gathering place for local folks. On the road connecting Philadelphia and Baltimore, a wayside tavern just west of Chadds Ford welcomed "Man and Horse." Built in 1714, the sturdy little hostelry still sits on the edge of "Ye Great Road to Nottingham," now the busy four-lane Route 1 highway.

Tavernkeeper William Barns, a blacksmith by trade, lived with his family on one side of the brick house and operated a public tavern in the other half. To revive the travel-weary, Barns dispensed beer, wine and other spirits from a caged bar that could be locked up after hours.

Overnight stays often meant sharing a bed with a stranger or sleeping on the floor. To give the family privacy, the two up-

15

A rare example of a colonial tavern that catered to travelers on the road between Philadelphia and Baltimore.

stairs bedrooms were not connected and a separate staircase led to each half of the house.

Barns was heavily in debt when he died in 1731. His widow Elizabeth, left penniless and with five children to care for, must have turned to drink. In 1763 the Kennett Quaker Meeting dismissed her, citing her tendency to "drink strong liquors to excess."

By 1753 James Brinton bought the house and farmland and it remained in the Brinton family for more than one hundred years. On the morning of September 11, 1777, General Knyphausen's troops marched past the front door on their way to Chadds Ford and the Battle of Brandywine. Joseph Brinton reported that British soldiers took two of his horses, a cow and other household goods.

The front of the tavern originally looked out over Route 1 until the highway was widened in 1938. The road was rerouted leaving the back of the tavern next to the highway.

Rescued from a state of disrepair by the Chadds Ford Historical Society in 1969, the Barns-Brinton House, as it is now called, shows what life was like in a rural colonial tavern and home. Four original fireplaces and much of the original wood paneling and hardware have survived. Tours and open-hearth cooking by guides in period costume are held May to September and by appointment.

The Battle of Brandywine

On September 11, 1777, an estimated 26,000 British and American soldiers swarmed over the peaceful countryside surrounding the Brandywine River and clashed in the largest land battle of the American Revolution. Chadds Ford residents found themselves in the path of the British campaign to capture Philadelphia.

The Battle of Brandywine lasted just one day — a day that ended in defeat for American commander-in-chief George Washington and his troops. Despite the loss, the battle bolstered American resolve as the colonials realized their fighting potential.

Although the British outmaneuvered Washington and marched on to occupy Philadelphia, they failed to capture or destroy the Continental army — a move that might have put an end to the colonial "rebellion." Moreover the American army's credible showing on the battlefield helped convince the young French General de Lafayette that the American cause deserved his country's support — a decisive factor in the defeat of the British four years later.

The impact of the battle on area residents was enormous. Property was destroyed during the fighting and afterwards the British took newly harvested crops, livestock, furniture, clothing, and whatever else of value they found.

To understand why and where the battle took place, how Washington was defeated, and what life was like for the 18th-century soldier, head to Brandywine Battlefield Park, one of Chadds Ford's premier attractions.

Brandywine Battlefield Park

Route 1, 0.7 mile east of Creek Road.
Info: (610) 459-3342; www.ushistory.org/brandywine

Brandywine Battlefield Park offers fifty acres of rolling, tree-shaded terrain on a high elevation that is pleasantly removed from the traffic below on Route 1. The Visitor Center provides an excellent overview of the battle with exhibits, maps and a video.

George Washington chose this location less than a mile from the Brandywine as his headquarters prior to the battle. The two Quaker farmhouses where Washington and the Marquis de Lafayette stayed while deliberating strategies are open to visitors.

Two days before the battle, Washington and his staff set up their command at the Benjamin Ring House, home of a prosperous Quaker miller. Built around 1720, the original stone colonial burned in 1931 and has been reconstructed and furnished to look as it did in 1777.

A short distance away Lafayette was quartered in the Gideon Gilpin House, a modest stone Quaker house built in 1745. Young, idealistic, and eager to fight the English, the 20-year-old Lafayette had volunteered his services and financial resources to the American government.

Washington quartered in a Quaker home near the Brandywine before the battle.

One of the oldest houses in Chadds Ford, the Gilpin house served as quarters for General Lafayette. The giant sycamore tree next to it dates back to Revolutionary times.

Washington's objective at Brandywine was to stop the British from advancing to Philadelphia, America's capital and most prosperous city. The stakes in the Philadelphia Campaign were high: the capture of the seat of the Continental Congress would have enormous symbolic value and disrupt the American war effort. The British hoped that freeing the city would rally Loyalist Pennsylvanians to their cause.

Washington chose to make his stand at the Brandywine River which offered a natural line of defense. He knew the British had launched a massive convoy of more than 260 ships from New York in late July. This formidable display of sea power was spotted sailing south along the Atlantic coast. Packed on board were an estimated 17,000 soldiers and over 300 horses, plus weapons, ammunition and supplies.

When the British discovered that the Delaware River — the direct route to Philadelphia — was fortified, the fleet sailed further south and up the Chesapeake Bay. On August 25 they disembarked in northern Maryland about 60 miles from Philadelphia. British General Sir William Howe's plan was to march overland and enter the American capital through the back door.

By September 9, the British had assembled a fighting force of about 13,000 at a camp in Kennett Square, Pennsylvania. Six miles away at Chadds Ford, Washington had positioned his main artillery high above the east bank of the Brandywine and posted guards at crossings up and down the river along a five-mile front. With limited supplies and a ragtag army of some 11,000 to 13,000 soldiers, patriots, and raw recruits, Washington prepared to face the most powerful army in the world.

As the sun set, American soldiers and officers gathered to hear the Rev. Jacob Troute recite a litany of British abuses and urge them to take up the sword for justice and right.

> *"The heights of Brandywine arise gloomy and grand beyond the waters of yonder stream, and all nature holds a pause of solemn silence, on the eve of bloodshed and strife of the morrow. . .My friends, I must urge you to fight by the galling memories of British wrongs. . . ."*
>
> — Sermon by the Reverend Jacob Troute, Sept. 10, 1777

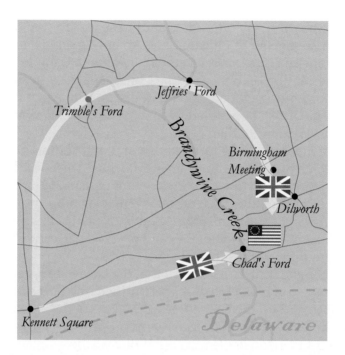

The actual fighting at Brandywine took place outside the Park boundaries — the fields of battle are now covered by housing developments and farms. History enthusiasts can buy a detailed self-drive tour map at the Battlefield museum shop that describes troop movements in the ten-square-mile Brandywine Battlefield National Historic Landmark. The Park also offers van tours of battle sites with a driver and guide.

For a quick overview, the top five battle sites can be seen on a short self-drive tour. What is remarkable is that many of the vistas look much as they did in 1777. The sites of the major action are in neighboring Birmingham Township which encompassed Chadds Ford at the time of the Revolution.

❖ *Insider's Tip:* As you follow this itinerary, note the many distinctive pre-Revolutionary era houses along Birmingham Road which was laid out along an old Native American path. Many of these 18th-century homes were built using an unusual greenish-color stone known as "serpentine" that was quarried nearby. Though beautiful in appearance, serpentine is a soft stone that disintegrates easily and is no longer used as a building material.

Following the Path of Battle: The Top Five Sites

1. Osborne's Hill: *British Lookout Point.*
Birmingham Road and Country Club Drive; historical marker on east side of the road.

On the morning of September 11, 1777, a heavy fog cloaked the Chadds Ford area. Near daybreak British Gen. Howe profited from that cover as he marched the majority of his troops northward rather than directly east towards Chadds Ford as Washington anticipated. Howe planned to cross the Brandywine further north, then loop around and surprise attack the Americans from the rear.

The remaining divisions, including thousands of professional German soldiers called Hessians who had been hired to fight in America, left camp a few hours later and marched straight up the

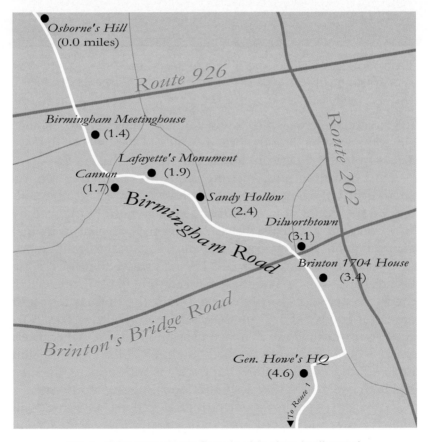

Map of Birmingham Road with sites indicated.

From Osborne's Hill General Howe could see American troops positioning themselves on the far ridge at Birmingham Hill.

road to Philadelphia which is now Route 1. They dug in positions along the west bank of the Brandywine at Chadds Ford directly across from the Americans and began trading artillery fire.

All morning long Washington heard conflicting reports about British movements to the north and delayed an all-out attack on the troops across the river. He had been outflanked by Howe on Long Island just the year before and was well aware that a repeat of that strategy could trap his troops at the Brandywine.

Meanwhile Howe marched his men above the forks of the Brandywine, well beyond the American right flank. Undetected, the Redcoats successfully crossed both the unguarded west branch at Trimble's Ford and the east branch at Jeffries' Ford. Circling southward, Howe marched past a mid-week Quaker meeting in Sconnelltown and reached Osborne's Hill on Birmingham Road around 2:00 p.m. Carrying weapons and supplies, the men had marched nearly 17 miles under hot, muggy conditions.

While the soldiers rested, the high elevation of Osborne's Hill offered Howe and his officers a sweeping overview of the terrain where the fighting would shortly begin.

". . .our eyes were caught on a sudden by the appearance of the army coming out of the woods into the fields. . . . In a few minutes the fields were literally covered over with them, and they were hastening towards us. Their arms and bayonets, being raised, shone as bright as silver, the sky being clear and the day being exceedingly warm. . . .

"Among[the principal British officers] was Gen. Howe. He was mounted on a very large English horse, much reduced in flesh, I suppose, from being so long confined on board the fleet. . . . The general was a large, portly man, of coarse freatures. He appeared to have lost his teeth, as his mouth had somewhat fallen in."

— Account of Joseph Townsend,
a young Quaker eyewitness, describing
the British arrival at Sconnelltown.

Some historians say Howe lost his opportunity for an all-out surprise attack on the Americans by "stopping for tea." However, Howe must have judged that his soldiers, having been on the move since before daybreak, needed to rest and refuel before fighting.

2. Birmingham Meeting House: *Battlefield Hospital.*
1245 Birmingham Road, opposite Meetinghouse Road.

Sometime after noon a local farmer, Squire Thomas Cheyney, rode into the American camp bursting with the news that he had spotted Redcoats marching to the north. Although the American officers were skeptical, Cheyney insisted he be allowed to speak directly to Washington. Further scouting reports soon proved Cheyney to be right.

Washington immediately sent troops to the high ground at Birmingham Meeting. The first shots were fired around 4:00 p.m. with the Americans rushing to close their line against the British attack. Philadelphia residents could hear the deep ominous sound of cannons firing thirty miles away!

The Quaker place of worship became the site of some of the bloodiest fighting in the Battle of Brandywine. American troops fired at the approaching British soldiers from behind the stone wall next to the meeting house.

The British with their greater numbers and the element of surprise on their side seized the upper hand. The defiant American response surprised the British who generally disparaged the rebels' fighting ability.

A simple granite block on the north side of the Birmingham Meeting House marks a mass grave for American and British soldiers.

Pacifist Quakers Caught in the Conflict

Because of their pacifist beliefs, Quakers (as members of the Society of Friends are called) did their utmost to remain neutral during America's fight for independence. But in 1777 war came to their doorstep. The wooden floorboards of Birmingham Meeting House were stained by blood when it served as a hospital for wounded soldiers. Before the battle the Americans commandeered it for their sick and afterward, the victorious British took it over and tended to the wounded from both sides.

> *"We hastened thither and awful was the scene to behold such a number of fellow beings lying near each other, severely injured and some of them mortally. . . . Some of the doors of the meeting house were torn off, and the wounded carried thereon into the house, which was now occupied as a British hospital. . . ."*
>
> — *Account of Joseph Townsend*

Built in 1763, the Quaker house of worship served as a hospital during the Revolution. Additions to the original meeting house were made in 1818 and 1968. Next to the meeting house stands an octagonal schoolhouse, built in 1819.

Local Quakers built the stone meeting house in 1763 to replace an earlier log meeting house. The building served as a center of community life and still has an active membership today.

In the 1700s the Quakers were the largest and most influential social group in Chester County. They had come to Pennsylvania as part of William Penn's "Holy Experiment," his vision of a free and tolerant society. These hardworking, plainly-dressed colonials owned prosperous farms and held positions of influence in the community.

When Americans began opposing British rule and fighting broke out, Quakers were caught in a moral dilemma. Their nonviolent beliefs prevented them from fighting or supporting the war effort in any way. By not supporting either side, however, the Quaker populace came to be viewed with suspicion or as traitors by both Americans and British.

They were fined for not joining the Pennsylvania militia and many lost their jobs for not signing an oath of allegiance. After the battle, the victorious British ransacked area farms but few Quakers reported their losses. Although in time they recovered economically, they never regained their former influence in local political affairs.

❖ *Insider's Tip:* Continuing south one-quarter mile on Birmingham Road, look for the cannon on the corner of Wylie Road. The iron cannon barrel is aimed toward the Osborne's Hill lookout of the British Commander in Chief.

3. **Lafayette Monument:** *Tribute to a Loyal Friend.*
    1311 Birmingham Road, 0.25 mile south of Wylie Road on left. (Note that the monument stands on private property and no parking is available.)

As the Americans fell back and were reforming their line, General Lafayette rode up from Chadds Ford and tried to rally the troops. In the chaos, the young Frenchman was shot in the leg — ending his first taste of combat in the Revolutionary War. A musket ball went straight through his calf and blood spilled over his boot. After his wound was dressed, he was transported to a hospital in Bethlehem, Pennsylvania, to recuperate.

Erected in 1895, Lafayette's monument honors the young French general who was wounded at the Battle of Brandywine.

Lafayette eventually returned to duty and forged a deep bond of friendship with Washington during the war. His loyalty to his commander and support for American independence earned him hero status among Americans. In 1824 he returned to America for a triumphal fifteen-month tour accompanied by his son, George Washington de Lafayette. Crowds cheered him everywhere.

Touring the battle sights at Brandywine moved him deeply as he recalled his youthful adventures. As he was driven down Birmingham Road, he got out of his coach and pointed to the place where he had been wounded. He put soil from the site into a bag that was buried with him when he died.

> *"When they came in sight of the Birmingham meeting-house, Lafayette arose in his carriage and addressed himself in French to his son and companions, spoke animatedly for some time, pointing out to them the different positions of the armies."*
>
> —Futhey and Cope, *History of Chester County*

In 1895 a column honoring Lafayette was placed at the site. Funded by the children of nearby West Chester, the monument was the first to commemorate the momentous events at Brandywine. In 2002, Congress awarded Lafayette honorary U.S. citizenship, a rare tribute.

4. Sandy Hollow Heritage Park: *Fiercest Fighting*.
Corner of Birmingham Road and South New Street.
Parking lot on South New Street.

A one-mile walking path encircles Sandy Hollow, the 44-acre field where American soldiers faced the British onslaught. As the Americans were pushed back from Birmingham Hill, Washington sent reserve troops who formed a line of defense at Sandy Hollow. Fighting was fierce: continuous musket volleys, bayonet charges and even hand-to-hand combat. This critical maneuver allowed time for American forces to make an orderly retreat and prevented the British from capturing the army in a rout. A cannon next to the walking path marks the center of the defensive line.

Back at Chadds Ford, British troops waded across the Brandywine and attacked the remaining American divisions. Despite a spirited defense, the Americans were outnumbered and forced to retreat.

By sundown, torn-up fields from Chadds Ford to Birmingham Meeting were littered with the bodies of some one thousand men. Bodies were buried where they had fallen. Although exact figures are not known, the British are believed to have suffered more casualties than the Americans.

A cannon stands along the west side of the walking path at Sandy Hollow, site of the final engagement of the Battle of Brandywine. It was placed there on September 11, 1900.

> *". . .How solemnly surges the Brandywine!*
> *Teeming with many a sorrowful sign—*
> *Heroes and horses, distorted and torn,*
> *Bloated and dead, on its surface upborne,*
> *Wounded ones writhing and wailing for aid,*
> *Fragments and missiles o 'er hillock and glade,*
> *Havoc and horror, disaster and night*
> *Palling the scenery and quenching the fight. . . ."*
>
> —*"The Brandywine"* by James B. Everhart

5. Dilworthtown: *The Path of Retreat.*

Intersection of Brintons Bridge Road, Birmingham Road, Old Wilmington Pike and Oakland Road.

As the sun set on September 11, thousands of American soldiers streamed through the village of Dilworth, as it was then called. Fighting continued until Washington, who galloped to the scene, ordered a retreat to the town of Chester some twelve miles away. With daylight fading and troops exhausted, the British chose not to pursue.

At midnight Washington wrote to Congress from Chester that morale was good despite the loss — a defeat he attributed to faulty intelligence:

> *"Sir:*
> *I am sorry to inform you, that in this day's engagement, we have been obliged to leave the enemy master of the field.*
> *. . . .But though we fought under many disadvantages, and were from the causes above mentioned obliged to retire, yet our loss of men is not, I am persuaded, very considerable, I believe much less than the enemy's.*
> *. . . .Notwithstanding the misfortunes of the day, I am happy to find the troops in good spirits; and I hope another time we shall compensate for the losses now sustained."*
>
> — *George Washington,*
> *letter to John Hancock,*
> *president of Congress.*

The British stayed on in the Dilworthtown area for five more days to treat the wounded and bury the dead. They also took their spoils: newly-harvested crops, food, furniture, livestock, clothing, and anything else they needed for replacement provisions. Village tavernkeeper Charles Dilworth reported a long list of "Wast Spoil & Destruction done and Committed by the Brittish army" that included three barrels of whiskey, 10 gallons of rum and 15 gallons of peach brandy!

Soldiers also looted personal possessions and wantonly destroyed property. Chester County suffered an estimated $1.6 million in property damage. The effect on the local economy was felt for years.

On September 26, a victorious Gen. Howe and his army marched into the American capital. The rebel Congress had escaped and would carry on the struggle for independence from outside Philadelphia. Washington would spend a bitter cold winter at Valley Forge rebuilding his army.

Known as the village of Dilworth during colonial times, this picturesque crossroads still has a cluster of historic structures. The village's namesake, blacksmith James Dilworth, built a red brick house here in 1758. His son Charles applied for a tavern

The crossroads at Dilworthtown stood in the path of the colonial retreat and its inn was ransacked by British soldiers.

license in 1770. For years the crossroads was known as "the Devil's half acre" for its rowdy clientele and drunken brawls.

The core of the brick house is now a part of the Dilworthtown Inn, a top-rated restaurant that serves gourmet fare in a beautifully-restored colonial setting. A blacksmith's shop, a former general store and several residences complete this historic complex.

❖ *Insider's Tip:* To see the house where British officers stayed after the Battle of Brandywine, continue south from Dilworthtown on Oakland Road to Harvey Road. Turn right and follow Harvey to where the road bends sharply to the right opposite Harvey Lane. The 18th-century house on the right served as Howe's headquarters and a hospital to treat the wounded.

Barn on Harvey Road. The winter of 1777 was a difficult one for the Chadds Ford residents whose farms had been looted by British troops.

Chadds Ford Painters And Poets

In the early 1900s N. C. Wyeth took summer painting classes in Chadds Ford, fell in love with its pastoral beauty, and eventually decided to settle there. The presence of the late N. C. Wyeth, his son Andrew, and grandson Jamie helped to create Chadds Ford's reputation as a thriving enclave for artists of the Brandywine Tradition. Since the opening of the Brandywine River Museum in 1971, Chadds Ford has gained international recognition as a venue for regional and American art.

Township Hall

Southwest corner of Route 1 and Ring Road, opposite
Brandywine Battlefield Park.
Info: (610) 388-6368; www.chaddsfordpa.net

Chadds Ford's celebrated artistic tradition began a century ago with summer painting classes held in Turner's Mill, also known Howard Pyle's Studio. The serpentine stone building, now the newly-restored Chadds Ford Township Hall, once provided a quiet retreat for a group of artists from Wilmington, Delaware.

From 1898 to 1903 illustrator Howard Pyle rented the mill and brought students from his Wilmington art school out to the country. Pyle was a highly respected illustrator in an era when illustrators were power players in the American media and in book publishing. Pyle painted on the second floor while his students worked below.

An avid history enthusiast, Pyle could gaze across the road to the stone house where George Washington headquartered during the Battle of Brandywine in 1777. The sight prompted him to paint *The Nation Makers*, his well-known work depicting a line of resolute young American patriots marching into battle, a tattered American flag held high. The 1903 painting now hangs in the Brandywine River Museum.

The shade of the huge sycamore tree next to the studio was no doubt a favorite gathering place for the artists during the heat of Chadds Ford summers. Old photographs show Pyle's students painting at their easels out of doors — men in coat and tie, women in high-necked blouses and long skirts.

Pyle's most talented protege was N. C. Wyeth, who was so taken with the setting that he later decided to make Chadds Ford his home. Pyle's followers gave birth to the Brandywine School of art and the Wyeth presence shaped Chadds Ford's artistic identity.

The former grist mill was built in 1867 by Joseph Turner, a wealthy Philadelphian. His large Victorian summer home "Windtryst" sat on the north side of the road. It was a time when "the Ford" was regarded as a fashionable summer place by city dwellers.

The mill was later converted to a residence but in the 1950s the inside was gutted by fire. In 1976 the township bought the building and 22 acres with the idea of converting the site to a recreational park. The project was shelved and the historic site sat vacant for 30 years. In 2006 the mill — completely renovated and with a new addition — was reopened as Chadds Ford's Township Hall.

Turner's Mill once provided a country retreat for Howard Pyle and his art students.

Chadds Ford Township Hall.

33

N. C. Wyeth House and Studio

Access is by shuttle bus from the Brandywine River Museum.
Info: (610) 388-2700; www.brandywinemuseum.org

When N. C. (Newell Convers) Wyeth found a site to build his Chadds Ford house and studio, the rising young illustrator described the location overlooking the valley as "the most glorious sight in this township for a home."

Wyeth bought the 18-acre property on Rocky Hill in 1911 for $2000. He and wife Carolyn had been living in Chadds Ford since 1908 in rented homes. A Massachusetts native, N. C. had strong ties with his family in New England and had toyed with the idea of returning there. However, in 1911 he was ready to put down roots and decided to settle his growing family permanently in Chadds Ford.

> *"I'm totally satisfied that this is the little corner of the world wherein I shall work out my destiny . . . here, I must acknowledge my soul comes nearer to the surface than any place I know."*
>
> — Letter from N. C. Wyeth to
> his parents, March 7, 1911

The income from his commission to illustrate the book *Treasure Island* gave N. C. the resources to build the house and studio he had been dreaming about for years. The conception and scale of the studio indicate that the 29-year-old artist was confident about his future prospects.

N. C. Wyeth became a prolific and highly successful illustrator who created memorable images for 112 books and thousands of magazine illustrations. Vigorous and adventuresome in his youth, he was of the perfect temperament to depict the heroes of adventure fiction. Although his paintings were inspired by the printed word, N. C. infused his work with a creative vision that often transcended commercial art.

A larger-than-life personality, he was a powerful presence in the world of illustration, the village of Chadds Ford, and most of all as head of his family. Educating their lively brood of five children at home, N. C. and his wife Carolyn sparked their imaginations and nurtured their talents. Andrew, Henriette (Hurd) and Carolyn became artists, Ann (McCoy) a composer and artist, and Nathaniel an inventor and engineer.

N. C. himself designed the family home, a spacious but unpretentious red brick and frame house with a front porch overlooking the valley. Two rooms are open to visitors. The "Big Room" was the family gathering place with family art on display. The small oak-paneled dining room has a long refectory-style table with benches for seating. A flagstone path at the back leads up the hill to N. C.'s workplace.

N. C. Wyeth designed his studio with a large north-facing Palladian window to provide proper lighting for his work.

The children spent many an hour playing, dressing up, or drawing in their father's studio with its soaring cathedral ceiling. The most striking feature of the studio is a graceful multi-paned Palladian window. N. C. designed the large north-facing window as a source of constant, steady light.

N. C. Wyeth died an untimely death in 1945 when his car stalled at the Ring Road railroad crossing and was struck by a train. His studio looks as it did on the day he died.

An unfinished portrait of George Washington sits on the easel. Nearby is his palette with dabs of oil paint that daughter Carolyn had kept and preserved. A canvas smock stiff with dried paint hangs on a hook. Displayed around the room are numerous props, costumes and artifacts that appear in his work.

After her parents died, Carolyn continued to live in the family home until her death in 1994. The Wyeth family then gave the property to the Brandywine River Museum so that visitors could see where so many memorable works in the museum were created.

The Brandywine River Museum

Route 1, just west of Creek Road.
Info: (610) 388-2700; www.brandywinemuseum.org

A former grist mill on the banks of the Brandywine has become a showcase for Wyeth art.

Wyeth art in the setting that inspired it — this winning combination has made the Brandywine River Museum the number one attraction in Chadds Ford.

Set in a verdant landscape on the banks of the Brandywine, the museum offers a Zen-like oasis of calm despite its location on busy Route 1. The core of the building is a 19th-century brick grist mill with harmonious additions giving the museum a fresh, contemporary feel. A three-stories-high glass wall offers a sweeping view of the river below.

When the Brandywine River Museum opened in 1971, the Wyeth family loaned many of its own paintings to flesh out the museum's modest collection of 20 artworks. The museum now owns more than 3,000 works of art and has had to expand the building twice to accommodate the growth.

The galleries' plaster walls, original wood beams and pine floors provide the perfect complement for the museum's collection of American art. The collection focuses on illustration, landscape painting, and still life, but its main drawing card is the Wyeth art.

The idea for the museum came about in the 1960s when the riverfront site was targeted for industrial development. A group of visionary area residents bought the property at auction. They formed the Brandywine Conservancy to protect the area's natural resources and preserve its cultural heritage.

The abandoned mill building seemed the perfect venue to display Brandywine art. Thanks to Andrew Wyeth's growing national recognition, the fledgling museum attracted 200,000 visitors the first year it opened.

Three Generations of Wyeths

Sorting out the many Wyeth family artists can be a challenge. The principal players are Newell Convers Wyeth or "N. C." (1882-1945), the famed illustrator and family patriarch; his son Andrew (born 1917), one of the most popular and influential painters in America today; and Andrew's son Jamie (born 1946), talented heir to the family legacy. Together they make up three generations of Wyeths who have lived in Chadds Ford and found it a source of inspiration in their work.

Although each has a distinctive style, they are considered part of the Brandywine School of painting that began with Howard Pyle's romantic realism. Despite his great success as an illustrator, N. C. yearned to break out of the confines of commercial art. During family vacations in Maine each summer, he experimented with various styles. But his large colorful canvases of historical and literary figures pulsing with drama remain his signature work.

"I started out painting at an easel but soon gave that up. It was too formal, too pat. I like to be in the scene I'm painting—sitting on a snowbank, lying in a marsh."

— Andrew Wyeth, *Autobiography*

After N. C.'s untimely death in 1945, Andrew took up the mantle of his father's work while developing his own artistic identity. No far-flung kingdoms of the imagination for Andrew: his realm was to be his own back yard — Chadds Ford and the coast of Maine.

His subdued palette of earth tones reflects these surroundings. His father, the only teacher he ever had, warned him that such somber compositions would not sell. Andrew not only proved that prediction wrong but found an audience at a time when realism was unpopular in art circles.

The youngest of the five Wyeth children, Andrew was clearly the most talented. As a child, he had poor health and was taught at home. Chadds Ford was his whole world and he wandered freely, observing and drawing. A feeling of solitude and even melancholy permeates much of his work.

Painting in watercolor and egg tempera, Wyeth is known for his meticulous brushwork and painstaking realism. A shape, a contrast, a color, a mood or something ephemeral might be the catalyst for his creative process. No detail is too insignificant for his attention.

Andrew Wyeth has spent a lifetime creating a highly personal pictorial legacy of the people, landscapes and buildings of Chadds Ford. Although much of that world has changed, his paintings continue to define Chadds Ford's image of itself.

Andrew and wife Betsy have two sons and from an early age Jamie displayed the family artistic talent. He left school at the end of sixth grade to devote himself to painting. Andrew's sister Carolyn became his teacher.

Despite the pressures of following a famous father and grandfather, Jamie has forged his own style, and is noted for his bold portraits of both people and animals. He achieved national recognition at age 21 with a posthumous portrait of President Kennedy. A crowd-pleaser in the museum collection is his well-known *Portrait of Pig*, depicting an enormous, pink, coarse-haired barnyard neighbor.

Jamie Wyeth at the Winterthur Point-to-Point races in Delaware.

He credits his grandfather's influence for the dramatic element in his work while his subject matter and composition is more akin to his father's. He devotes most of his time to painting either in Chadds Ford or his island home in Maine.

"Inspiration is overrated. I push myself. Once in a while things really start clicking. That's the opiate."

— Jamie Wyeth interview

Frolic Weymouth: Chadds Ford Visionary

Founder and chairman of the Brandywine Conservancy, accomplished artist, du Pont family heir, George (Frolic) Weymouth is Chadds Ford's best-known mover and shaker. Weymouth was just 31 years old when he formed the Conservancy and began his lifelong advocasy of environmental causes. The Conservancy's mission is to protect the integrity of the rural landscape depicted by the Brandywine artists — a daunting challenge given the value of remaining open land in the area.

Weymouth, an accomplished landscape and portrait artist, has also been instrumental in the founding and growth of the Brandywine River Museum which is operated by the Conservancy.

Weymouth's Chadds Ford home, "The Big Bend," sits on over 200 acres of pristine rolling land overlooking the Brandywine. The core of his old stone house dates back to 1640 when Swedish settlers built a trading post by the stream to trade with the Lenape Indians.

Weymouth is also known for his collection of antique carriages — museum-quality pieces he uses and enjoys. A highlight of the annual Winterthur Point-to-Point steeplechase is the arrival of the parade of antique carriages with Frolic and his smartly-dressed party in the lead.

Kuerner's Farm

Ring Road, 0.4 mile south of Route 1. Access is by shuttle bus from the Brandywine River Museum.

Info: (610) 388-2700; www.brandywinemuseum.org.

The home of a hard-working German immigrant couple named Karl and Anna Kuerner has become an iconic image of Chadds Ford, thanks to artist Andrew Wyeth. For close to 70 years Wyeth has depicted the Kuerners, their farm, barn, cattle, and views of their property — a total of more than 1000 works. Tourists from all over come to see the farm that has become so well known through Wyeth's paintings.

As a child, Wyeth discovered he could walk from his house over the hill to Ring Farm as it is also known. The Kuerners emigrated from Germany in 1926 and rented the farm for 14 years until they had saved enough to purchase the property.

Wyeth first painted there in 1932 at age fifteen, and the Kuerners eventually gave him free rein to draw and paint as he pleased. Enduring images of Karl in his World War I military uniform, his wife Anna, and the old farmhouse are among Wyeth's most famous works.

Kuerner's Farm has become an iconic image of Chadds Ford through Andrew Wyeth's paintings.

In 1986 Wyeth startled the art world when he exhibited 240 paintings and drawings he had done of Helga Testorf, a German woman who helped care for the aging Karl Kuerner. The intimate portraits of a nude Helga, done over a period of fifteen years, fueled speculation about the relationship of the artist and his muse.

After both his parents died, Karl Kuerner, Jr. donated most of the 33-acre farm in 1999 to the Brandywine Conservancy, the nonprofit organization that operates the Brandywine River Museum. The Conservancy purchased the remaining acreage and opened the historic farm to visitors. Karl Jr. continues to grow hay on the property which is one of the last working farms in Chadds Ford.

Victoria Wyeth: Family Historian

For a unique perspective on Wyeth art, join Andrew Wyeth's granddaughter Victoria on one of her popular gallery tours at the Brandywine River Museum. An engaging speaker, she regales visitors with family anecdotes and insights she has gained from conversations with her grandfather about his art and creative process. Call the Museum for Victoria's tour schedule at (610)388-2700.

Bards and Balladeers

From 19th-century romantic to contemporary bard, poets and writers have distilled and described the Brandywine experience in highly personal terms. In the late 1800s and early 1900s romantic poets such as James B. Everhart, John Russell Hayes, and Thomas Buchanan Read wrote in idyllic terms about the Brandywine's beauty and historical significance.

Continuing this tradition, Chadds Ford singer/songwriter Sally Jane Denk melds a lifelong interest in history with a gift for music. A performer at many local events, Sally evokes America's past in a clear, soprano voice. *Bard of the Brandywine* reflects her Quaker philosophy of looking within as a way of knowing God and oneself.

Folksinger Sally Jane Denk
at Chadds Ford Days.

> *"A younger child would look in awe at those of gentle fame*
> *Of poetry and songs and lore, I longed to have their name.*
> *Then one day in a meadow green, I found with joyful glee*
> *The Bard upon the rustic stage was no one else but me!*
> *And now I sing my song for you, my heart in every line*
> *This place has made my life complete, the Bard of the Brandywine."*
>
> — Fourth verse, *The Bard of the Brandywine*, © 1992

Born in England, Sonia Ralston is a Chadds Ford writer and poet who writes insightfully about history, the land, and the rituals of everyday life. For 31 years Ralston lived with her family in the 1839 Edward Brinton house overlooking the Brandywine. When the time came to scale down, she wrote in her newspaper column in *The Kennett Paper* about the leaving her historic home in "Goodbye to the old house."

> *"The real mourning came later, just as I knew it would. There are still early spring days — moist and magical — when I grieve I can no longer search for those first unfailing snowdrops whose whereabouts I knew so intimately!. . . .*
> *Does a house have a soul? I like to think so. We were merely its temporary custodians, and those walls will stand long after we are dust. But our laughter and our dreams . . . our ups and downs . . . became a small part of its fabric forever... just as there remained something of all those generations which had gone before."*

Chadds Ford Village

At the turn of the last century Chadds Ford Village had two railroad stations, a creamery, a lumber and coal yard, carriage works, two general stores, grange hall, two churches, a harness shop, a barber shop and drugstore according to historian Chris Sanderson. A number of white frame houses from that era are still standing on Creek Road and Station Way Road.

Looking south on Creek Road.

The Brandywine was spanned by a covered wooden bridge built in 1860. One mile upstream another covered bridge spanned the Brandywine at the mill at the end of Brintons Bridge Road. Two general stores did a thriving business, selling groceries and a little bit of everything else. Baldwin's Store was next to the Chadds Ford Hotel. A second general store, Gallagher's Country Store, was located on the corner where Leader's Sunoco station now stands on Route 1 at Station Way Road.

Heyburn Road railroad bridge.

That road led to the Chadds Ford Station, a stop on the Philadelphia and Baltimore rail line. Just west of the Brandywine River at Chadds Ford Junction, passengers could board the Wilmington and Northern line. After the railroads were built in the mid-1800s, summer tourists began to come out to "the Ford" from Wilmington and Philadelphia. Wealthy people built summer homes along Baltimore Pike (Route 1).

The surrounding countryside was mostly rolling fields and pastures dotted with farmhouses and barns — family farms were the backbone of the local economy. Along the Brandywine's banks, mills converted the area's abundant resources into marketable products. Powered by the stream's currents, the mills ground grain, sawed wood and made paper — and provided jobs and income for many local residents.

> "...The old farmsteads upon thy grassy slopes
> Are homes of a contented people, proud
> to till the acres which their fathers held
> Ere that red day on Birmingham's high hills.
> Here old-time faith and manners are not dead;
> Calm days and nights fill out the tranquil year;
> Simplicity hath here her dwelling-place,
> And all is pastoral happiness and peace. ..."
>
> — *The Brandywine,* by John Russell Hayes

45

Old Township Hall

Station Way Road.
Info: (610)388-6368; www.chaddsfordpa.net

Until 2006 local government in Chadds Ford was housed in a quaint white frame building that for fifty years was a village church. Old Township Hall began life as St. Luke's Episcopal Church around 1885. Photographs from the early 1900s show the little church, minus the front porch, with the entrance from the road flanked by a low stone fence.

When the congregation dwindled to a handful of people in 1934, the church was sold and converted to a four-room private residence. In 1977 the township bought the building for $7,000 and converted the interior to one large meeting room with a beamed ceiling.

Every month Chadds Ford's three-member Board of Supervisors meets to discuss issues such as open space, zoning, development and routine administrative matters. Depending on the issue, meetings can be sleepy or packed with residents. Land development is especially controversial. Most residents are eager to preserve the township's vanishing landscape, while developers covet any property with a Chadds Ford address.

The former St. Luke's Episcopal Church.

Archie's Corner

Corner of Ring and Bullock Roads, 0.6 mile south of Route 1.
Limited parking.

Many Chadds Ford residents who drive by the ruins of Mother Archie's church know little of its curious and controversial history. Fewer are aware that Chadds Ford once had a thriving African-American community.

The one-room Bullock School was built around 1838 using an octagonal design that was popular at the time. Pupils' desks were arranged facing the windows with the teacher keeping an eye on things from the middle. After a new school was built nearby, the Bullock School closed in 1875. Preacher Lydia A. Archie bought the building in 1891 and held religious services there for the local black community.

Known as Mother Archie or Sister Archie, she lived in a frame house adjacent to the church and carried on her ministry until she died in 1932. Mother Archie and her parishioners were part of an African-American community in Chadds Ford established by local Quakers after the Civil War.

The two simple structures sitting on what was then a remote corner in Chadds Ford caught the eye of a young Andrew Wyeth early on. Over the years he did many paintings and drawings of the eight-sided church and members of the black community he came to know as friends.

The corner of Ring and Bullock Roads remains a peaceful last resting place for Sister Archie and some of her parishioners.

The crumbling walls of the old church, the house's foundation and a scattering of tombstones are all that remain on the half-acre property now owned by Chadds Ford Township.

The fact that church members were buried on the property fueled a dispute in the 1950s between the township and descendants of Archie's parishioners. The property had been seized by the county because of delinquent taxes and a new buyer donated the land and deteriorating buildings to the township.

Descendants of Archie's followers petitioned to have the property returned because they had relatives buried there. The court ruled against them. Plans to build a town hall on the site never materialized, probably because of the expense of rehabilitating the building.

Christian C. Sanderson Museum

1755 Creek Road, just north of Route 1; parking across the road.
Info: (610) 388-6545; www.sandersonmuseum.org

Born in 1882, Chris Sanderson became a kind of unofficial mayor of Chadds Ford. Everyone knew him and he knew everything about Chadds Ford. He was a teacher, a lecturer, a fiddler, and a square dance caller. But above all else, he was passionate about history and preserving Chadds Ford's past.

Sanderson collected everything he could get his hands on related to Chadds Ford, Americana, history, or his own life experiences. His mind-boggling collection of over 40,000 artifacts is displayed in the little white house on Creek Road where he once lived.

Sanderson's first home in Chadds Ford was the Washington Headquarters house where he lived with his mother from 1906 to 1922. At that time the property that is now Brandywine Battlefield Park was still in private hands.

Sanderson liked nothing better than telling people about the battle or showing them his collection of historical artifacts. He hung a "Welcome Visitors" sign on the front fence and in 1921 alone hosted more than 9,000 visitors. His mother would offer pie baked in the big fireplace to guests. No admission was ever charged — their only motive was to make people more aware of America's heritage.

Sanderson was worried that Chadds Ford's legacy might slip away one building and tree at a time. He was devastated when the Washington Headquarters house burned down in 1931 after he and his mother had moved away. He promoted the idea of turning the battlefield into a state park which eventually happened in 1952.

> *"He was a fixture on the highways — never raised a thumb — just stood there with fiddle case and brief case in hand and cars would stop. I believe that's the way he traveled all over...."*
>
> Florence Betts Brosch,
> Chadds Ford Historical Society Oral History Project

Founding curator Tommy Thompson on the front porch of the museum.

Money was unimportant to Sanderson, and he and his mother often struggled to make ends meet. He lost his teaching job in 1929 and eked out a living as a lecturer and square dance teacher.

When Sanderson and his mother were evicted from a house in Pocopson for failure to pay rent, N. C. Wyeth found them the house on Creek Road and offered to cover the rent if necessary.

Sanderson collected both trash and treasure, filling the eight-room house from floor to ceiling with antiques, artifacts, newspapers, and memorabilia. When he died in 1966, his longtime friend and biographer, Tommy Thompson, helped sort through the chaos and organize the collection.

From the piles emerged original drawings by N. C. and Andrew Wyeth, historical artifacts from the American Revolution and Civil War, autographs and letters, and arcane bits of Americana.

Andrew Wyeth spearheaded the drive to keep the house and Sanderson's collection as a museum. Sanderson's old friend, Tommy Thompson, served for years as curator of the collection and still often may be seen welcoming visitors to the house.

The Sanderson Museum's vast and varied collection includes a portrait of Chris Sanderson by Andrew Wyeth entitled "Chris."

Hank's Place

Corner of Route 1 and Creek Road.
Info: (610) 388-7061

Located on the northwest corner of Chadds Ford's main intersection, the small restaurant known as Hank's is a neighborhood favorite where a cross-section of Chadds Ford society rubs elbows with one another. People love the unpretentious atmosphere, the home-style food and reasonable prices. The restaurant's personable owners, Peter and Voula Skiadas, added a covered porch several years ago to shelter customers who line up to wait for a table on busy weekends.

Behind the counter at Hank's, grillman Bill Lynch with Voula and Peter Skiadas who describe the restaurant as "a place where carpenter belts and attache cases sit side by side."

The large menu includes homemade soups, sandwiches, Pennsylvania Dutch specialties like pork and sauerkraut plus Greek dishes from the Skiadas' native Greece. The restaurant's popular breakfast specials — served all day — include a shiitake mushroom omelet that Gourmet magazine once described as "a breakfast standard and a tour de force."

The location of Hank's Place next to the Brandywine has a long tradition as a local gathering place — first as the site of a blacksmith's shop, then a vegetable stand and an open lunch stand. When the Skiadas' bought the eatery in 1991, they kept the name Hank's, which harks back to previous owner Hank Shoupe who owned the restaurant in the 1960s.

Baldwin's Store: Selling a little bit of everything

One of two general stores in Chadds Ford a century ago, Baldwin's Store occupied the large rambling building next to the Chadds Ford Inn. Originally the store had a mansard roof and was similar in design to the Inn. The large general store with its broad front porch occupied half of the building and sold groceries and other necessities. The Chadds Ford post office was also located there. The Baldwin family lived on the other side. Their thirteen-room home had nine bedrooms and a bath.

A devastating fire in 1915 destroyed the store and several other adjacent buildings. The rebuilt general store that opened in 1920 featured the "Battle Field Tea Room" and a meeting hall. The recently-renovated Baldwin's houses a cafe and take-out store.

Chadds Ford Inn

Route 1, just east of Creek Road.
Info: Brandywine Prime Seafood & Chops @ Chadds Ford Inn
(610) 388-8088; www.brandywineprime.com

The Chadds Ford Inn with its broad front porch has been the site of a hotel or tavern for over two centuries. At the time of the Battle of Brandywine, the proprietor was Joseph Davis. In his petition for a tavern license in 1772, Davis described the location as "formerly John Chads' where a tavern has been for thirty years" — though the exact location of that tavern is the subject of debate.

The present Georgian-style stone inn was built in the early 1800s. The inn changed hands many times and was known variously as the "Rising Sun," the "Bridge Inn" (after the first bridge was built) and the "Chad's Ford Tavern". In the 1830s, a group of local residents tried (unsuccessfully) to have the inn closed down complaining that their hired help spent too much time there "in the company of the dissipated and profane."

After the railroads were built in the mid-1800s, the Chadds Ford Hotel did a brisk business catering to summer tourists and artists.

"Next to my father's house [Baldwin's Store] was the hotel. What an attractive place it was!

. . . I admit there were a few Baptists that did not think a hotel necessary for a village.

You entered the hotel through the front door. To the right was a large living room, dining room, kitchen and pantry. To the left was the bar and another room with small tables surrounded by chairs.

In the fall and spring the artists often stayed in this hotel. I loved the place and I'm sure it was well managed or my parents would not have allowed the Passmores to have me over so often."

— Mabel Baldwin Lawrence,
My Childhood Days in Chadds Ford

This historic Inn has been a Chadds Ford landmark for more than 200 years.

Around 1940 new owners purchased the hotel which had sat empty for several years. Extensive renovation work was done, including removing the stucco that covered the exterior stonework. The hotel had eight small guest rooms. Regulars in the dining room included the Wyeth family, Chris Sanderson and people coming out to Chadds Ford for a meal in the country.

In 2007 a completely refurbished Inn was reopened as Brandywine Prime featuring contemporary ambience and cuisine within the centuries-old stone walls.

Chadds Ford Historical Society

1736 Creek Road, 0.25 mile north of Route 1.
Info: (610) 388-7376; www.chaddsfordhistory.org

When several of Chadds Ford's landmark historic properties were targeted for sale in the 1960s, local residents were spurred into action. The grassroots effort to save and restore the deteriorating John Chads house — home of Chadds Ford's ferryman namesake — gave birth to the Chadds Ford Historical Society in 1968.

The group raised enough money to buy the Chads house and four acres for $25,000. A year later they scrambled to buy a dilapidated pre-Revolutionary tavern sitting vacant on Route 1 — today the handsomely restored Barns-Brinton House.

At first the tiny springhouse below the Chads house served as the Society's meeting place. In 1991 the group built a new headquarters designed to resemble a Pennsylvania stone bank barn. It was constructed on the site of the former Hoffmann dairy barn opposite the John Chads house.

Today the Society is one of Chadds Ford's largest community-based organizations with hundreds of local residents and history enthusiasts involved in its operation and events.

History enthusiasts of all ages help out at Society events.

The Chadds Ford Historical Society is housed in "The Barn," adjacent to the John Chads House (above) and springhouse (below).

The Society's focus is the social history of Chadds Ford with emphasis on the 1700s. The history of Chadds Ford is told through tours and demonstrations by costumed guides at the two historic houses. The Barn features exhibits, lectures and a research library. To fund their educational programs, the Society sponsors annual events such as Chadds Ford Days, the Great Pumpkin Carve and Candlelight Christmas in Chadds Ford.

Living in Chadds Ford: The Doctor's Daughter

Florence Betts Brosch was the youngest of four children of Dr. William Betts and his wife Edith. The Betts moved to Chadds Ford in 1906 and lived in the Victorian house on Route 1 opposite the Brandywine River Museum's parking lot.

"Father's rounds were made first by horse-drawn buggy if the weather allowed. During flood season he would go by horseback — and in snow by sleigh. . . . He never billed anyone. He did accept services — washing, ironing, dress making; also chickens, turkeys, eggs — even a muskrat!"

The Brandywine was a focus of activity with swimming and canoeing in the summer and ice skating and sledding in the winter. One especially vivid memory, Brosch says, was the arrival each summer of a large caravan of gypsies who would set up camp by the Brandywine.

"One time I was in [Gallagher's] store when gypsies were there. A gypsie lady spread a napkin on the counter and asked him to hold a handful of bills — not change — over it. He complied and, believe it or not, she somehow, without touching, brought bills down on that napkin."

Chadds Ford as I Remember It,
Florence Betts Brosch,
Chadds Ford Historical Society Oral History Project

Brandywine Baptist Church

Route 1, 1 mile east of Creek Road.
Info: (610) 459-1302

Located on several acres at the edge of Brandywine Battlefield Park, little Brandywine Baptist Church has its roots in Quak-
erism. A small log meetinghouse was built on the site in 1718 by
a group of Quakers who had broken away from the Society of
Friends. The group met in private homes beginning in 1692 making it the second oldest continuous Baptist congregation in Pennsylvania. A stone church replaced the log church in 1808. The
present classical revival church was built in 1869 with tall arched
windows gracing a simple sanctuary.

A long-held church tradition is baptism by total immersion
in water performed at the banks of the Brandywine — a practice
a few hardy souls still opt for today. In the past a changing house
was built near the stream for the use of those being baptized.

In the late 19th century a row of sheds was built along Route
1, providing hitching facilities for twenty carriages. A stepping
stone used by parishioners to get into their carriages still stands
close to the highway.

The church's first parsonage, a Victorian house built by the
men of the church in 1883, is located at the corner of Route 1 and
Heyburn Road.

Quakers who split off from the Society of Friends were the
founders of Brandywine Baptist Church.

Chadds Ford Elementary School

Route 1, west of Creek Road.
Info: (610) 388-1112; www.ucf.k12.pa.us

The Chadds Ford Consolidated School was built in 1925 on a ten-acre site just west of the Brandywine. Up until then local children attended eight one-room rural schools scattered about Chadds Ford, Birmingham and Pennsbury townships.

Some of these quaint buildings are still standing today. One example is the Brinton's Bridge School, a brick building with a small front porch built in 1903 at the northeast corner of Brinton's Bridge Road and Creek Road. Another schoolhouse, built in the classic octagonal design in 1889, is now part of a private home on the southwest corner of Heyburn and Ridge Roads.

A former one-room octagonal schoolhouse now part of a private home. Heat was provided by a woodstove in the middle of the room.

The new red brick Chadds Ford School cost about $110,000. Pierre S. du Pont of Longwood Gardens funded nearly half the project because his large staff at Longwood was the source of much of the school's population growth. The school opened with 264 students in grades one through ten, with one teacher for each grade.

In 1954 Chadds Ford consolidated with Unionville to relieve overcrowding. Chadds Ford became an elementary school and students traveled to Unionville for high school. Plans to close down the aging school in the late 1990s met strong opposition from the school's many supporters, and a major renovation was undertaken in 2002.

Thanks to the artistic influence in Chadds Ford, the school has had a strong arts program. Jamie Wyeth attended school there for six years in the 1950s. A wonderful collection of original art hangs on the walls of the school, including works by seven Wyeth family members, Rea Redifer, Peter Hurd, Howard Pyle, George Weymouth, Paul Scarborough and other prominent Brandywine artists. The annual Chadds Ford Art Show held each spring at the school features works by some of the most popular Brandywine artists.

A painting from the school art collection, May Day, *by Chadds Ford artist Paul Scarborough, depicts a long-standing school tradition.*

Brandywine Summit Camp Meeting

Beaver Valley Road, 0.5 mile west of Route 202.

Hidden away in the woods just north of the Delaware state line, the Brandywine Summit Camp Meeting began as part of the American religious revival that took place after the Civil War. Eight Methodist churches from Pennsylvania and Delaware established the camp meeting in 1866 as a place to gather for worship and recreation in the summer. They leased the 13-acre site with its towering beech and oak trees from farmer William Johnson (whose farmhouse is now the Brandywine Conference and Visitors Bureau at Route 202).

At first the campers stayed in canvas tents but soon they started building cabins side by side. Today 75 little painted cabins — some more than 100 years old — are clustered around the large open tabernacle that was built in 1884. At the height of the movement, there were well over one hundred cabins and many families spent the whole summer at the camp. Most came from Wilmington and West Chester seeking Christian worship and fellowship — and an escape from the summer heat. Some families arrived by horse and carriage, others took the train from Wilmington that ran north along the Brandywine. The camp provided a getaway for middle-class Americans who could not afford an expensive resort. Amenities included a grocery, ice cream and candy stores, and a full agenda of inspirational speakers and recreation.

Every year since 1866 people have gathered at Brandywine Summit, making it the longest continuously running camp meeting on the East Coast. The camp association bought the property in 1943. Today the camp is Christian non-denominational and many cabins are owned by people whose families have been coming there for generations.

Built side by side, the cabins surround an open
tabernacle that is the focus of camp activity.

Chadds Ford Today

Despite its proximity to traffic-clogged arteries and the fact that its main street is now a four-lane highway, much of Chadds Ford has retained an idyllic sense of place. The days of walking to the village are gone, but neighbors still catch up on the news at the post office, the convenience store, or gas station.

Some of Chadds Ford's image of itself stems from Wyeth art, some from the events that give people a sense of community. Chadds Ford's annual events and traditions are much-anticipated occasions for visitors and residents alike. With quaint antique shops, galleries, wineries and a nice selection of restaurants and lodging, Chadds Ford has become a popular getaway destination.

Chadds Ford off the beaten path.

A rustic building housing the post office, a bank, and convenience store is at the center of "downtown" Chadds Ford.

Chaddsford Winery

Route 1, 1.8 miles west of Creek Road.
Info: (610) 388-6221; www.chaddsford.com

Since its founding in 1982, Chaddsford Winery has brought a bit of Old World ambience to Chadds Ford. Visitors to the estate winery, housed in a colonial-era dairy barn, can sample various vintages, tour the cellars, and learn about winemaking.

Proprietors Eric and Lee Miller chose to settle in Chadds Ford believing that southeastern Pennsylvania's moderate climate and fertile soil offered conditions amenable for growing wine grapes. Few shared their vision at the time!

Winemaker Eric Miller monitors one of his barrel-aged wines.

This did not deter Eric Miller, whose own father had moved the family to France to learn about winemaking while Eric was growing up. When the family returned to the U. S., Eric's father started up a winery on the family farm in the Hudson Valley.

Today Chaddsford is the largest and best known winery in Pennsylvania and winemaking has become serious business with more than 100 wineries in the state. The Millers' quest to make distinctive regional wines has earned them increasing national respect. Varietals including chardonnay, merlot, pinot grigio, cabernet and pinot noir are sold in wine stores and served in restaurants from New York to Washington.

The winery is especially lively in summer with a popular Friday night concert series and several wine festivals. Concertgoers bring picnic fare, sample wines and relax to music in the winery's outdoor courtyard.

Chadds Ford Post

Read all about what's happening in Chadds Ford in the weekly Chadds Ford Post. *The community newspaper began as a one-page experiment in 1998 and evolved into a full-fledged newspaper in 2001. Editor Richard Schwartzman is well known in the community and personally covers all government meetings and local events.*

S. I. W. Vegetables

Creek Road, 2 miles south of Route 1.

One of very few operating farms remaining in Chadds Ford, Hill Girt Farm spans 700 acres of rolling hills on Route 100 along the Brandywine. In the summer people brake for sweet corn, tomatoes, and other vegetables at the little S. I. W. ("stepped in what?!") roadside stand. Farmer H. G. Haskell III grows a cornucopia of different vegetables for his loyal summer clientele plus supermarkets and restaurants.

One crop stands out, however: the giant 400-plus-pound pumpkins he grows each year for the annual Pumpkin Carve at Chadds Ford Historical Society. He supplies some 70 pumpkins for the event and it takes a three-man crew to hoist each monster squash from barn to truck. The famous pumpkin crop has even inspired art — Haskell was surprised one day to find artist Jamie Wyeth in his pumpkin patch working on a painting now titled "Hill Girt Farm."

The farm has been in the family since 1910 when H. G.'s grandfather, Harry G. Haskell, bought the property and operated a dairy farm. Before that, the farm had been owned by the Joseph Pyle family for a hundred years. Part of the barn dates to the 1600s when the property was first settled, according to Haskell.

The roadside stand at Hill Girt Farm attracts corn connoisseurs in summer.

The picturesque stone building near the fruit stand is the former Cossart train station built by Haskell's grandfather. Trains once carried passengers and freight along the route between Coatesville and Wilmington.

Transporting one of H.G. Haskell's prize pumpkins is not a one-man job.

Chadds Ford Days

Chadds Ford Historical Society, Creek Road, 0.25 mile north of Route 1.
Info: (610) 388-7376; www.chaddsfordhistory.org

Each September, Chadds Ford celebrates its colonial heritage at the annual Chadds Ford Days. Held in the meadow behind the Chadds Ford Historical Society, the two-day event features scores of traditional craftspeople selling their wares, a colonial tavern, food from area restaurants, live music and kids' activities.

The tradition began in 1958 when local residents got together to commemorate the Battle of Brandywine. Dressed in colonial garb, they held a parade, art show, and a square dance. Over the years the hometown celebration was held from time to time as a salute to Chadds Ford's heritage.

In 1968 a nine-day Chadds Ford Days fair was organized to raise money for the restoration of the John Chads house. The event was held in the old grist mill that was to become the Brandywine River Museum. Exhibits of colonial lifestyles, Wyeth art, and a mock battle on the Brandywine attracted 25,000 visitors.

By 1970 Chadds Ford Days had become an annual weekend event sponsored by the Chadds Ford Historical Society. It continues to attract visitors from all over.

Colonials feel right at home at Chadds Ford Days.

Summertime on the Brandywine.

Hill Girt Farm.

Revolutionary Times

Brandywine Battlefield Park, Route 1, 0.7 mile east of Creek Road.
Info: (610) 459-3342; www.ushistory.org/brandywine

Chadds Ford's most momentous historical event is brought to life every year at "Rev Times" — a reenactment of the Battle of Brandywine held in September. Cannons boom and muskets smoke as American troops defend against invading Redcoats. The spectacle is staged on the rolling terrain of the Battlefield Park where Washington and Lafayette headquartered during the actual battle in 1777.

The two armies set up camp in the Park along with female "camp followers" who prepare meals and mend uniforms. The scene brings to mind the daunting challenge Washington must have faced in outfitting, feeding, and transporting supplies for 15,000 soldiers on the march in colonial America.

The day-long event also features musket and rifle demonstrations, children's activities, colonial merchants and crafts, and historical talks and exhibits.

The Great Pumpkin Carve

Chadds Ford Historical Society, Creek Road, 0.25 mile north of U. S. Route 1.
Info: (610) 388-7376; www.chaddsfordhistory.org

A unique and very popular event, the three-day Great Pumpkin Carve features some 70 knife-wielding artists who transform giant gourds into fabulous creatures, scenes and Halloween themes. The specially-grown pumpkins — some topping over 450 pounds — are assigned to artists randomly. Carvers decide on the spot how to incorporate an odd shape or imperfection into their design.

American troops face the formidable Redcoats each
September at Brandywine Battlefield.

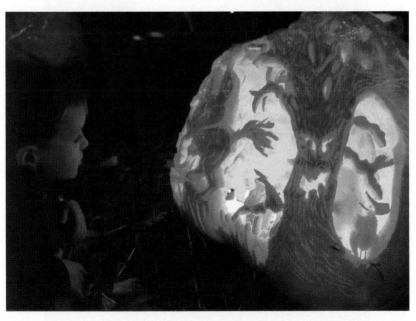

Children are mesmerized by the haunting spectacle at the Great Pumpkin Carve.

At nightfall when the carving is completed, the pumpkins are lit and judges award prizes in various categories. Crowds file through the darkness past the finished masterpieces, children staring wide-eyed at the eerie spectacle.

The carving competition usually takes place on the Thursday evening before Halloween, with the lighted pumpkins on display Friday and Saturday evenings. Rounding out the festivities are hayrides, live music, and hot food on all three evenings.

The pumpkin-carving tradition in Chadds Ford began in the 1970s when a few local artists gathered on the porch of the Chadds Ford Inn around Halloween for a spirited competition. As word spread, the crowds grew and in 1992 the Carve was moved to the meadow behind the Chadds Ford Historical Society.

Christmas in Chadds Ford

'Tis the season to see Chadds Ford decked in its holiday finery, sometimes with a dusting of snow to soften the starkness of a Brandywine winter. That has not always been the case as early Quakers did not "celebrate" Christmas and went about their usual business on December 25.

A Brandywine Christmas

Brandywine River Museum, Route 1, late November through early January.
Info: (610) 388-2700; www.brandywinemuseum.org

Holiday visitors flock to the Brandywine River Museum each year to see the annual Christmas display of trees and trains. The display in the ground-floor lobby features Christmas trees covered with whimsical "critters." The all-natural ornaments are made by an army of volunteers who collect unusual seeds, pods, and plant material all year long to make as many as 9,000 ornaments a year for display and sale. A popular collectible, the critters have even adorned trees at the White House and The Smithsonian.

Upstairs, families watch model trains run over mountains and through villages on over 2,000 feet of track in an elaborate room-size display. Also featured is a Victorian dollhouse with rooms filled with miniature furniture. Special art exhibits with winter or holiday themes are featured in addition to the permanent collections in the Andrew Wyeth and Brandywine Heritage Galleries. The wall of windows overlooking the Brandywine River offers a beautiful winter backdrop, especially when snow is on the ground.

Fuzzy critters festoon the
trees at the Museum.

Christmas in Miniature

The Chadds Ford Gallery, Chadds Ford Village and Barn Shoppes, Route 1.
Info: (610) 459-5510; www.awyethgallery.com

While shoppers elsewhere stand in line for the latest fad or toy, in Chadds Ford they line up for art — especially at the opening of the annual Christmas in Miniature show at The Chadds Ford Gallery. This popular event features small original framed works by some fifty established artists. Oils, pastels, and acrylics, all no larger than twelve by fourteen inches, are reasonably priced beginning at under $100.

Barbara Moore readies the gallery for its annual show of small paintings.

Gallery director Barbara Moore, the doyenne of the local art gallery scene, came up with the idea in 1982 as a way of making original art affordable for young collectors. Now young and old crowd into the small gallery each year to find that perfect gem among the hundreds of miniature works that cover the walls.

The gallery, which specializes in regional art and Wyeth reproductions, occupies a rustic brick farmhouse built in 1859. The farm's former outbuildings house quaint gift shops.

Candlelight Christmas in Chadds Ford

Info: Chadds Ford Historical Society (610) 388-7376;
www.chaddsfordhistory.org

The self-drive Candlelight Christmas tour offers a chance to visit some of Chadds Ford's most distinctive homes — all candlelit and decked in their holiday finery. Held the first Saturday in December, the tour features three to four private homes plus several historic sites with special holiday presentations and light refreshments.

Colonial holiday traditions at Barns-Brinton House.

Antique Christmas decorations and family heirlooms create a magical holiday ambience at the home of Dave and Judy Murtagh.

Christmas in the Meadow

Route 1, meadow opposite the Chadds Ford Inn — check posted sign for date and time.

Shortly before Christmas, Santa Claus stops to visit the children of Chadds Ford. What keeps children guessing is how he will arrive — by sleigh, in a carriage, by helicopter, truck or fire engine, or perhaps on horseback. Santa keeps everyone in suspense until he appears, usually at 1 p. m. the Saturday before Christmas. The Brandywine Lions Club, which arranges Santa's visit, prepares hot chocolate and goodies for the children and their families.

Longwood Gardens

Route 1 at Route 52, 4 miles west of Creek Road.
Info: (610) 388-1000; www.longwoodgardens.org

For many, no holiday season is complete without a visit to Longwood Gardens, described by London's Financial Times as "the best Christmas display in the world." Located just west of Chadds Ford, Longwood's world-famous horticultural gardens are spectacular in every season but a must-see at Christmas. Lines of cars start creeping into the parking lot at dusk when the thousands of lights on Longwood's trees begin to shimmer against the darkened sky. Inside the Conservatory, acres of colorful poinsettias, towering fir trees, flower gardens, and exotic plants delight the eye and revive the spirit. Organ and choral concerts, fountain displays, and special cultural programs, are held throughout the season.

Dining in a Historical Setting

Brandywine Prime Seafood & Chops @ Chadds Ford Inn
>Route 1, just east of Creek Road; Tel: (610) 388-8088; www.brandywineprime.com.
>A contemporyary dining experience with New American cuisine in a centuries-old Chadds Ford landmark.

The Chadds Ford Tavern and Restaurant
>Route 1, 1 mile east of Creek Road; Tel:(610) 459-8453.
>Tavern fare in a cozy, comfortable setting with lots of Brandywine art.

The Gables
>Route 1, 1.5 miles west of Creek Road; Tel: (610) 388-7700; www.thegablesatchaddsford.com.
>A nineteenth-century dairy barn reborn as a stylish restaurant with imaginative menu.

The Dilworthtown Inn
>1390 Old Wilmington Pike, Dilworthtown, Tel: (610) 399-1390; www.dilworthtown.com.
>The three-story Revolutionary War-era inn offers gourmet dining, superb wine cellar and attentive service in a historic, candlelit setting.

The Mendenhall Inn
>Route 52, 1.5 miles south of Route 1; Tel: (610) 388-1181; www.mendenhallinn.com.
>Fine dining on the site of the eighteenth-century Mendenhall family farm.

Chadds Ford Information

Lodging, Restaurants, Shopping, Calendar of Events

Brandywine Conference and Visitors Bureau
Route 202 and Beaver Valley Road.
Info: (610) 565-3679; www.brandywinecountry.org

Chester Country Conference and Visitors Bureau Visitors Center
Route 1 at entrance to Longwood Gardens.
Info: (610) 388-2900; www.brandywinevalley.com

www.thebrandywine.com
An on-line guide to hotels, restaurants, shopping, recreation.

www.bvbb.com
Brandywine Valley Bed and Breakfasts: a listing of historic
lodgings with all the amenities.

Sources and Further Reading

The Chadds Ford Historical Society.

The Chester County Historical Society.

Ashmead, Henry Graham. *History of Delaware County*. Philadelphia: Louis H. Everts, 1884.

Everhart, James B. *Poems*. Philadelphia: J. B. Lippincott, 1868.

Futhey, J. Smith and Gilbert Cope. *History of Chester County*. Philadelphia: Louis H. Everts, 1881. Source of quotes by Joseph Townsend.

Hayes, John Russell. *The Collected Poems of John Russell Hayes*. Philadelphia: The Biddle Press, 1916.

James, Arthur E. *A History of Birmingham Township*. West Chester, PA: The Chester County Historical Society, 1971.

Lawrence, Mabel Baldwin. *My Childhood Days in Chadds Ford*. Media, PA: Thomas B. T. Baldwin Sr., 2001.

McGuire, Thomas J. *Brandywine Battlefield Park: Pennsylvania Trail of History Guide*. Mechanicsburg, PA: Stackpole Books, 2001.

McMullan, Mary W. *A History of the Development of Chadds Ford School 1916-1980*. Copyright 1980.

Mowday, Bruce. *September 11, 1777*. Shippensburg, PA: White Mane Books, 2002.

Ralston, Sonia. "Goodbye to the Old House." *The Kennett Paper*, June 26-July 2, 1997.

Brandywine Battlefield Park Commission. *The Brandywine Spirit*. Copyright 1975. Source of sermon by the Rev. Jacob Troute.

Thompson, Thomas R. *The Washington's Headquarters Story*. Copyright 2002.

Fitzpatrick, John C., ed. *The Writings of George Washington from the Original Manuscript Sources 1745-1799*. Available online at http://etext.lib.virginia.edu.

Wyeth, Betsy James, ed. *The Letters of N. C. Wyeth, 1901-1945*. Boston: Gambit, 1971.

Wyeth, Andrew. *Autobiography*. Boston: Little, Brown, 1995.

Wyeth, Andrew. *Close Friends*. Mississippi Museum of Art. Jackson: 2001.

About the Author

Carla Westerman is a writer, journalist and photographer who has lived in the Chadds Ford area for more than 20 years. From 1997 to 2001 she covered Chadds Ford for *The Kennett Paper* writing feature stories and news.

A native of Pennsylvania, she has a deep interest in 18th-century American history and serves on the board of the Chadds Ford Historical Society. Her family tree includes four men who served in the Revolutionary War — one of whom drove George Washington's personal supply wagon.

Carla and her husband Richard live in Birmingham Township and have two grown children.

THOMAS PUBLICATIONS publishes books about
the American Colonial era, the Revolutionary War,
the Civil War, and other important topics. For a
complete list of titles, please visit our website:

http://thomaspublications.com

Or write to:

THOMAS PUBLICATIONS
P.O. Box 3031
Gettysburg, PA 17325

Chadds Ford barbershop sign painted by N. C. Wyeth,
Sanderson Museum.